JUV/E8
SF
75.5
.F367
2004

EASTSI

Chicago Public Library

W9-ACL-313

Farm animals

CHICAGO PUBLIC LIBRARY
VODAK EASTSIDE BRANCH
3710 EAST 106 STREET
CHICAGO, IL 60617

DK READERS

Pre-level 1

Fishy Tales
Colorful Days
Garden Friends
Party Fun
In the Park
Farm Animals

Level 1

A Day at Greenhill Farm
Truck Trouble
Tale of a Tadpole
Surprise Puppy!
Duckling Days
A Day at Seagull Beach
Whatever the Weather
Busy Buzzy Bee
Big Machines
Wild Baby Animals
A Bed for the Winter
Born to be a Butterfly
Dinosaur's Day
Feeding Time
Diving Dolphin
Rockets and Spaceships
My Cat's Secret
First Day at Gymnastics
A Trip to the Zoo
I Can Swim!
A Trip to the Library
LEGO: Trouble at the Bridge
LEGO: Secret at Dolphin Bay
A Day in the Life of a Builder
A Day in the Life of a Dancer
A Day in the Life of a Firefighter
A Day in the Life of a Teacher
A Day in the Life of a Musician
A Day in the Life of a Doctor
A Day in the Life of a Police Officer
A Day in the Life of a TV Reporter
Gigantes de Hierro *en español*

Level 2

Dinosaur Dinners
Fire Fighter!
Bugs! Bugs! Bugs!
Slinky, Scaly Snakes!
Animal Hospital
The Little Ballerina
Munching, Crunching, Sniffing, and Snooping
The Secret Life of Trees
Winking, Blinking, Wiggling, and Waggling
Astronaut: Living in Space
Twisters!
Holiday! Celebration Days around the World
The Story of Pocahontas
Horse Show
Survivors: The Night the Titanic Sank
Eruption! The Story of Volcanoes
The Story of Columbus
Journey of a Humpback Whale
Amazing Buildings
Feathers, Flippers, and Feet
Outback Adventure: Australian Vacation
LEGO: Castle Under Attack
LEGO: Rocket Rescue
¡Insectos! *en español*
Ice Skating Stars

A Note to Parents

DK READERS is a compelling program for beginning readers, designed in conjunction with leading literacy experts, including Dr. Linda Gambrell, Director of the Eugene T. Moore School of Education at Clemson University. Dr. Gambrell has served on the Board of Directors of the International Reading Association and as President of the National Reading Conference.

Beautiful illustrations and superb full-color photographs combine with engaging, easy-to-read stories to offer a fresh approach to each subject in the series. Each DK READER is guaranteed to capture a child's interest while developing his or her reading skills, general knowledge, and love of reading.

The five levels of DK READERS are aimed at different reading abilities, enabling you to choose the books that are exactly right for your child:

Pre-level 1: Learning to read
Level 1: Beginning to read
Level 2: Beginning to read alone
Level 3: Reading alone
Level 4: Proficient readers

The "normal" age at which a child begins to read can be anywhere from three to eight years old, so these levels are only a general guideline.

No matter which level you select, you can be sure that you are helping your child learn to read, then read to learn!

Chicago Public Library
Vodak/East Side Branch
3710 E. 106th St.
Chicago, IL 60617

LONDON, NEW YORK, MUNICH,
MELBOURNE, AND DELHI

Series Editor Deborah Lock
Designer Sadie Thomas
U.S. Editor Elizabeth Hester
Production Alison Lenane
DTP Designer Almudena Díaz
and Pilar Morales
Jacket Designer Simon Oon

Reading Consultant
Linda Gambrell, Ph.D.

First American Edition, 2004
04 05 06 07 08 10 9 8 7 6 5 4 3 2 1
Published in the United States by DK Publishing, Inc.
375 Hudson Street, New York, New York 10014

Copyright © 2004 Dorling Kindersley Limited

All rights reserved under International and Pan-American Copyright Conventions. No part of this publication may be reproduced, stored in a retrieval system, or transmitted in any form or by any means, electronic, mechanical, photocopying, recording, or otherwise, without the prior written permission of the copyright owner.

Published in Great Britain by Dorling Kindersley Limited

Library of Congress Cataloging-in-Publication Data
Farm animals.-- 1st American ed.
p. cm. -- (DK readers, pre-level 1)
ISBN 0-7566-0536-9(pbk) ISBN 0-7566-0534-2 (hbk)
1. Livestock--Juvenile literature. I. Dorling Kindersley readers. Pre-level 1, Learning to read.
SF75.5.F367 2004
636--dc22

2004007457

Color reproduction by Colourscan, Singapore
Printed and bound in China by L Rex Printing Co., Ltd.

The publisher would like to thank the following for their kind permission to reproduce their photographs:
a=above; c=center; b=below; l=left; r=right t=top;

www.agripicture.com: Peter Dean 22–23. **Alamy Images:** Bildagentur Geduldig/archivberlin Fotoagentur GmbH 18-19; Jack Sullivan 26-27. Ardea.com: John Daniels 10-11. **Corbis:** Darrell Gulin 8-9; Kit Houghton 24-25; Randy M. Ury 4-5. **DK Picture Library:** Barleylands Farm Museum and Animal Centre 6, 8–9, 16; Philip Dowell 12, 14, 15, 18; Jerry Young 15; Tracy Morgan 15; Odds Farm Park 19; Barrie Watts 20, 21. **Getty Images:** Pal Hermansen 20t; Hans Reinhard 11t. **Holt Studios International:** 15t. **Oxford Scientific Films:** Mark Hamblin 14-15; Konrad Wothe 12t.

All other images © Dorling Kindersley
For further information see: www.dkimages.com

Discover more at
www.dk.com

DK READERS

LEARNING TO READ
pre-level 1

Farm Animals

DK Publishing, Inc.

R0404757001

feathers
chickens

Here is the chicken
with her little chicks.

Here is the turkey
coming to meet you.
beak
turkeys

feathers

Here is the pig.
Here are three
pink piglets.

pigs

ear

Here are the cows looking at you.

hoof

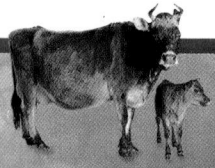

COWS

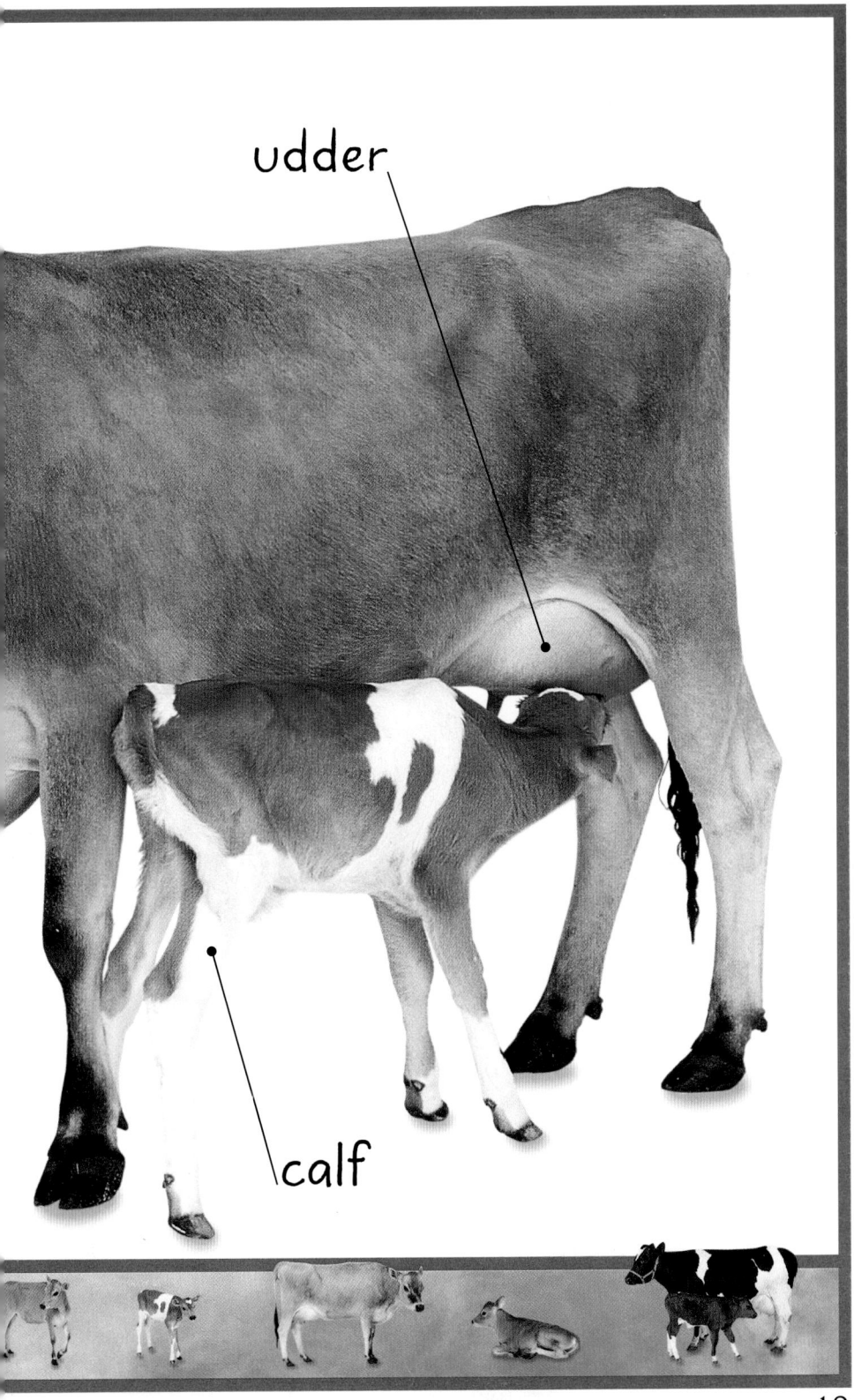
udder
calf

Here is the dog.
Here are three
sleepy puppies.
nose
puppy
dogs

Here are the sheep with a little lamb.

sheep

wool
ear

nose
goats

Here is the goat
lying down
with her kid.

Here are the ducks
with their
fluffy ducklings.

ducks

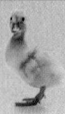

beak
duckling

Here are
the white geese
looking all around.
geese

eye
neck

Here is the horse
running with her foal.

horses

mane

ponies

Here are two
little ponies.
pony

Here is the cat
curled up with
her kitten.

cats

hay
ear

Come see us
again soon!

Which animal

Neigh!
o you like best?

Picture word list

chicken
page 6

turkey
page 8

pig
page 10

cow
page 12

dog
page 14

sheep
page 16

goat
page 18

duck
page 20

goose
page 22

horse
page 24

pony
page 26

cat
page 28